The Identity of "AngiArts"

By Angi Perretti

Cover
"Fantasy Swan" Monument
A Monument for Artistic Inspiration
Lake Eola Orlando
Third Millennium AD 21st Century
Circa 2008

FOR MILLENNIA THE POWERFUL ART GODS HAVE WAITED
IMPATIENTLY FOR THE UNIVERSE TO PROVIDE
THE LONG-AWAITED ONE—
A MUSE FOR ARTISTIC INSPIRATION!

THE IDENTITY OF "AngiArts"
21st Century   2008   3rd Millennium AD

Copyright © 2018 The Identity of "AngiArts"   © All Rights Reserved.

First Edition Published September, 2008
Second Edition Published June, 2016
Third Re-Publication June, 2018

ISBN # 978-0-692-14425-1   HC
ISBN # 978-0-692-14426-8   SC
ISBN # 978-0-692-14442-8   E-Pub

No part of this book may be reproduced, stored in a retrieval system, or transmitted by any means without the written permission of the author.

Angi Perretti
Costume Designer / Arts & Culture Philanthropist / Author
The Identity of "AngiArts"©   The Chronicles of Angi Perretti©
Swans of the World Habitats©
"Fantasy Swan"™ Monument at Lake Eola
Cottage Way, Downtown Orlando, Florida
"AngiArts"® is the 10th Identity Trademark Design of
"Walking~Works~of~Art"™ Collections
www.angiarts.com

Genre
PER013000   Live Theatre Operetta Musical / Performing Arts Productions
FIC009100   A Fantasy Escape for Culture Book Lovers
ANT005000   A Letterbox Adventure for Sculpture Art Enthusiasts

Credits
Caricature image "AngiArts"® by Derek Smith, Sunshine Photographics.
Caricature cartoon landscape by Henry Flores Graphics.
Front Cover sculpture image by Shirley Bolin Photography.
Fantasy Swan" images by Shirley Bolin Photography.

Published and Printed in the United States of America by:

MCrc Industries, LLC
A Publishing House
Oakland, Florida USA
2018

The Identity of "AngiArts"

By *Angi Perretti*

Illustrations By Stephen Adams

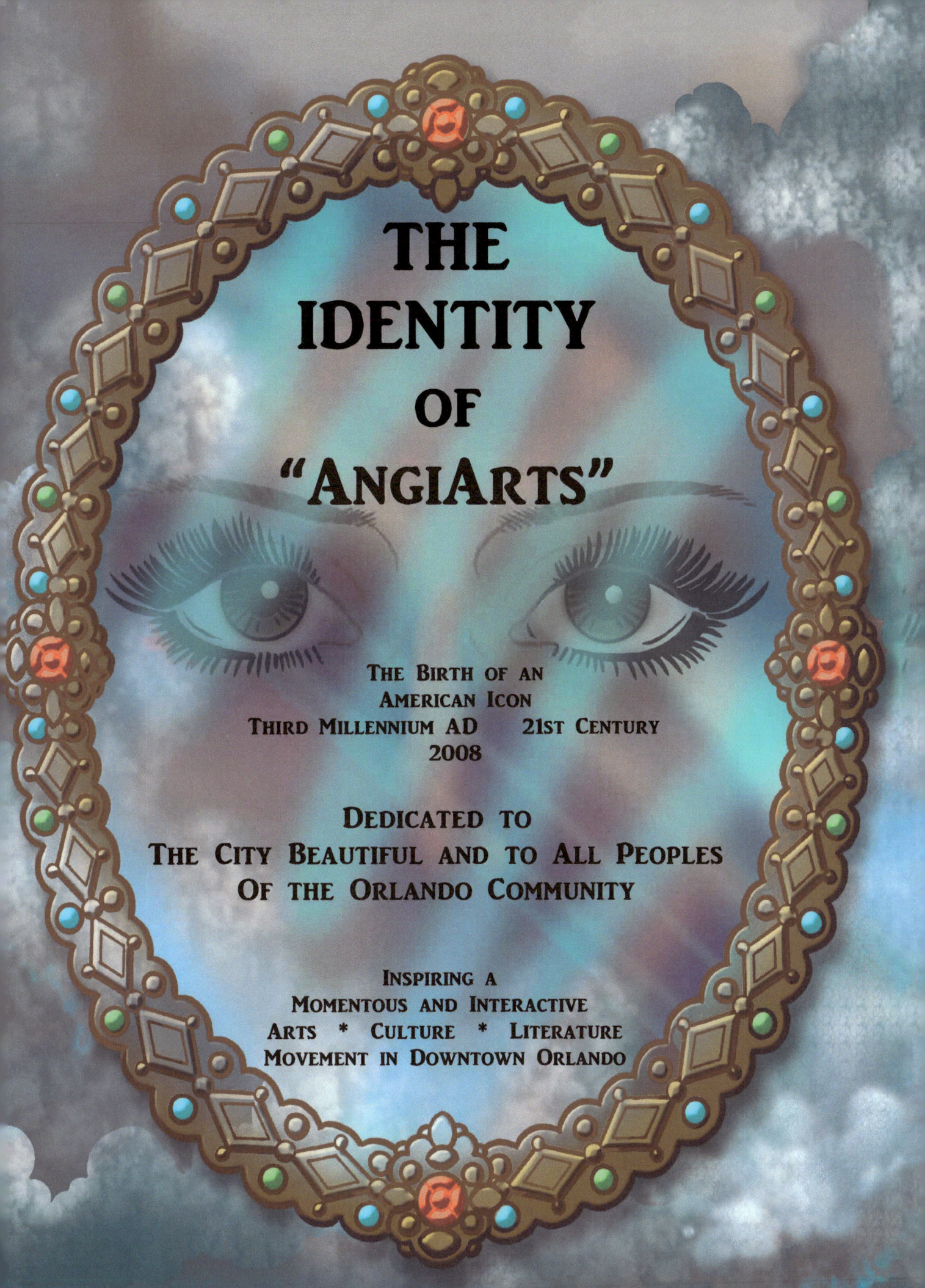

ACKNOWLEDGMENTS

"AngiArts" celebrates and joins the collective efforts of our vibrant arts community, which includes all leaders of the City Beautiful and the numerous arts and cultural resources, organizations, and patrons who continuously cultivate Orlando's cultural ambience. Together, we are presenting a world-class *City for the Arts* to central Floridians and to all honored visitors from around the world.

"I look forward to becoming an instrumental participant in promoting Orlando to a world-class arts community! Over the years, I have come to affirm that Orlando is just the most exciting city in Florida to enjoy life at its best. I believe Orlando possesses a kindling spirit for a flourishing art community that beckons and welcomes a broad spectrum of artists."

INTRODUCTION

GREETINGS!
ALL PEOPLES OF THE THIRD MILLENNIUM AND THE ORLANDO ARTS & CULTURE COMMUNITY:

Let me tell you how excited I am to present this book to you.....This story was so much fun to write that I actually got caught up in a wild and creative frenzy that defied all sanity! It all started back in May 2006, when I published one of my identity trademark designs in the *Orlando Arts Magazine*. Her name was "AngiArts." Since then, I feel like I have been actually living this identity in real life. This powerful force of intellect and inspiration totally motivated me to react with this exaggerated literary response…unimaginable till now!

The Identity of "AngiArts" is a modern-day legend that stages the fictitious life and identity transformation of a twenty-first-century *comic-book-style* cartoon character for the Arts. I created her with the sole intention to rally and promote the current arts and culture movement in downtown Orlando. The story narrates her fairy-tale life before the reality of her current presence—where she came from and how she got here; who she is today and why she landed in downtown Orlando.

Adopting mythical legends and incorporating magical mysteries of the fairy tales of olden days, the story depicts an unusual mixture of literary elements recognizable to fairy-tale readers. However, this fable underscores pertinent plot and character references symbolic to my life, and references the hardships and struggles that we all may face in the quest for truth and purpose in our own lives.

The fantasy characters symbolize real-life family members, and each one has relayed a unique element of truth to me during his or her life. However, all of them directly affected my own personal identity transformation to the designer and artist I am today. During the writing process, I found myself reviving my deepest childhood fantasies and fondest memories, while at the same time, reliving my darkest sorrows. I am grateful for all their precious memories.

So here we go, Everyone…

Imagined and founded upon the fertile dreams of a little farm girl from Miami, this whimsical fantasy transcends reality via fairy-tale format, but then launches forward at literary warp speed into a fanciful plot that introduces "AngiArts"—a present-day cartoon caricature of the author.

Get ready for a wild ride through literary art!

The Identity of "AngiArts"

The Inaugural Adventure of
The Chronicles of Angi Perretti
Third Millennium AD
Volume I   21st Century
2008

INSCRIPTION

"Hear Ye...Hear Ye...Now I will begin to tell you the story of "AngiArts"—a twenty-first-century art zealot with superpowers. The missions of her destiny are perpetual adventures."
A.P.

Once upon a time, a long time ago in a far, faraway land of Orient glory...

A time when ancient royalty ruled kingdoms for thousands of years...

A time when legends abound with the mystical mystery of magic potions and powerful genies...

A time when folklore portrayed its fantasies through the storytelling of magicians and the prophecies of sorcerers...

A time when following the stars and interpreting dreams as divine messages from God became a powerful world that existed beyond the senses, utterly defying the existence of reality...

There lived a very famous king with his faithful queen.

CHAPTER ONE

King Melchior's Kingdom

King Melchior (mel´-key-or) built his Great Clay Castle of Persia with pride and surrounded it with sculpture gardens filled with fragrant flowers, songbirds, and crystal ponds. King Melchior was well known in his kingdom because he was one of the three Magi who followed the star in the east to bring gifts of gold to a newborn King lying in a manger.

Besides duties as ruler of his palace, King Melchior was a talented sculptor who could hand-carve a statue right out of solid rock from the mountain sides and pour liquid bronze through molds he made from clay. King Melchior was a kind and generous king, who was so wealthy that he gave gold coins to everyone in his kingdom, especially if they were poor. Because of his generosity, famine and disease never descended upon King Melchior's land. He was well loved. He ruled his kingdom with compassion. Everyone respected and honored this great king. His word was more solid than gold, for he always held himself accountable for whatever promises he made.

This king was highly favored by God. His royal family was blessed with the riches of love and happiness, more valuable than gold. King Melchior honored his beautiful Queen Helena very much. She was a hardworking and patient person. Queen Helena taught her princess daughter to always sit up straight, for one day she too would be sitting on a throne. Her steadfastness, grace, and femininity exalted the grandeur of the kingdom. The queen was very elegant and admired by all throughout the lands.

Princess Angilika (an-gee-lee´-ka) was the only daughter of the royal couple. King Melchior loved his princess with *eyes of happiness*. These royal parents nurtured Angilika in love, and sheltered her from all things evil. King Melchior was very proud of his daughter because she handcrafted all his royal robes with the finest fabrics of velvet and brocade. Princess Angilika was the only one in the kingdom who was allowed to sew his royal wardrobe. The little princess relished her noble identity and lived many years in the creative fulfillment of her natural talents.

Because this royal couple could no longer bear any more children, King Melchior presented his noble queen with a flock of magic swans. These sacred creatures reigned over all the crystal ponds inside the palace gardens. This made Queen Helena very happy. Princess Angilika took care of her mother's royal swans, naming each one, and even making them elegant necklaces of satin, ribbons, and jewels. The queen was especially content to spend time with Princess Angilika as she fed the magic swans down by the pond. The little princess fell in love with one of the swans that had a black neck and pink feet, just because it looked different from the rest. She named it, "Queenie," after her mother. Her beautiful pet swan floated effortlessly with grace and elegance upon the crystal ponds. Princess Angilika always wanted to be just like her.

In those days, legends told that magic swans were sacred caretakers for truth and hope. Angilika had always desired Queenie's mystical charms, and she would spend hours confiding in her down by the pond's edge. So, Angilika would reveal her deepest desires to Queenie and ponder the many obstacles that stood in the way of her quest to seek her soulful identity. She wanted to discover the purpose for her birth.

As Princess Angilika grew older, she believed feverishly that her soul's identity was subliminal to her human identity. She resolved herself to always seek truth and purpose in her life, no matter what obstacles altered her pathways. Peacefully, her sacred swans were always awaiting nearby to listen to the voice of her heart.

The Magic Swan Flock

CHAPTER TWO

The Voice of Her Dreams

Angilika lived a very happy childhood. Very often, Angilika would daydream all day about creating elaborate gowns for opera queens and traveling the kingdoms in search of the finest fabrics and jewels. And very often at night, she would have one certain dream over and over again. It was the voice of her dreams, revealing her destiny and promising the answers to her many questions. She always felt happy inside her dreams and very excited to trust her imaginings.

As time went by, she began to despise their constant arrival in the middle of the night. In fact, her dreams continuously tormented her because her joy and excitement always led to grave disappointment whenever she awoke the next morning. She always believed that her dreams would someday come true, and she hoped that more ways to fulfill her gifted talents were waiting to be revealed by the stars. But her impatience was now becoming a constant source of sadness for Princess Angilika. How could something so happy make her so sad and disappointed?

Divine Messages from God

Now it came to pass one night, Princess Angilika had another very vivid dream. But this time its message was urgent. The voice called out to her, *"Do not be afraid, Princess Angilika, for God's grace is upon you. Your petitions have been heard and I have been sent to bring you this good news. You must obtain a divine prophecy from the Phantom Prophet. He has the answers you need to discover your soul's identity and the purpose for your birth. You must release your inner being. She is the angel of your soul and the wings to your destiny. Behold, when these things come to pass, your soul shall become immortal to fulfill your purpose on earth."*

Before Princess Angilika could speak back to the voice, something woke her up. It felt like someone touched her hair. The urgency of the voice's instructions kept her up the rest of the night. The next morning, the princess ran to tell her father about the voice in her dream. She was so excited that she pleaded with her father to send for this Phantom Prophet at once. He was the kingdom's only spiritual director.

The king became very upset at Princess Angilika's request. In those days, evil sorcerers were greatly feared because they often performed dangerous spirited spells using powerful witchcraft tricks that delivered their subjects into a vast oblivion. The king knew it was quite possible she would fall into an everlasting sleep. He was afraid for his princess, and he quickly refused. But the princess persisted and begged her father to do so.

"Please, Father, I will seek the angel of my soul, even if it means that I must face grave danger and fear. I will not succumb to sorcerer evil, for the goodness in my heart shall repel any evil spell placed upon me. Father! This might be my only chance! We must follow the voice's instructions!" begged Angilika.

King Melchior reluctantly gave in, for he loved his precious daughter so much that he would do anything for her. He admired his daughter's determination and courage to search for truth and purpose amid the forces of evil. She learned that from him. He immediately sent out the palace messengers to summon the Phantom Prophet. However, little did she know that she was about to encounter another one of life's internal battles between good and evil.

LETTERBOOK NOTES

Did you ever have a dream that was so real, it woke you up from a happy sleep?

_____
_____
_____
_____
_____
_____
_____
_____

CHAPTER THREE

The Phantom Prophet

When evening came, the kingdom's spiritual sorcerer arrived at the Great Clay Castle after several days' journey out from the desert where he lived. The Phantom Prophet was of great age and arrived clothed in dusty robes of black and white. A hood covered his pointed head and weathered face, shielding it against the desert winds. His deep, dark eyes appeared so sullen and shadowy that he frightened the king and Princess Angilika. Queen Helena begged to send him away.

"I am here, My Lord. What shall be your command?" the mysterious Phantom Prophet spoke in reverence.

Ignoring this fearful sight, the king said, "My princess daughter was given a message in a dream that only you can help us seek the angel of her soul. I command you to guide us to this truth. Work your magic potions upon her."

"My Lord, you have been told of my witchcraft deeds and spirited spells against the forces of evil. Under my spells, if your princess has lived a dishonest life, her soul could turn black and she may never rise again."

Abruptly, the king threatened him in a loud voice. "I COMMAND YOU TO SECURE HER BLESSED SOUL! THE CASTLE DUNGEONS ARE DARK AND THE RATS SHALL DEVOUR YOUR FLESH! YOU SHALL NOT ALLOW ANY HARM TO BEFALL MY DAUGHTER!"

Princess Angilika turned to her mother and father with a loving, reassuring glance and said, "I have lived a happy life with you. I have always lived this life with honesty in my heart and love within my soul. Oh, my royal

parents, please do not be afraid. Cast away your fear. We shall conquer this moment together."

Overcome by the terror of imprisonment, the Phantom Prophet begged for mercy. "My Lord, if this is Princess Angilika's moment of destiny, my potions will not betray her blessed soul. Hereby, I warn you. Your precious daughter must follow my instructions carefully."

Undaunted by fear and upheld by the voice in her dream, the princess was eager to follow the prophet's instructions. She nervously glanced over to his very large trunk covered with red desert dust. It held everything he needed to put her under a very dangerous spell. As her worried parents looked on, the Phantom Prophet began his devious ritual. He mixed the magic potions and swirled their wicked ingredients around and around. When he poured the mixture into a silver chalice, its hot, mystical steam rose above the cup like a thick forest fog. He gave the cup to the princess. As soon as her lips touched the liquid potion, she immediately dropped to her knees.

King Melchior glared at the wretched sorcerer's face. He saw that the Phantom Prophet's bewitching spell was upon his precious daughter. He could hardly contain his fright. In his weakest moment, he struggled to maintain a strong faith in the truth he was about to receive. Queen Helena prayed for her daughter's soul and pleaded for the presence of all three arch angels to surround her daughter.

The Phantom Prophet reached deep inside his trunk again and took out an elaborate mirror rimmed with gold leaf and jewels. Its magic glass was invisible, and only those under his spell could see through it. He placed the magic mirror in her hands, and raised the silver chalice high above her head. Its foggy mixture descended upon the princess. Silence prevailed.

After a few moments of stillness, he spoke. "Your eyes are the windows to your soul. This magic mirror will let you see through your eyes and directly into your soul," he instructed. "Peer deeply within your soul, my little one. Your angel will appear. Your soul's identity awaits your discovery."

Princess Angilika could feel a cool, misty breeze blowing past her face. Sweet fragrances of roses and lilies surrounded her body. A peaceful feeling came over her. Just then, the mystical powers of the prophet's mirror took over. Angilika's own reflection flickered and disappeared, but what reappeared seconds later stunned her. Suddenly, she was astonished to find herself peering into the eyes of a most beautiful angel!

The Magic Mirror

At once, the angelic being identified herself. *"Do not be afraid, for behold, I am the Angel of the Eastern Star. I once led your father, King Melchior, and the Magi safely out of harm's way. Rejoice and be glad! I am the voice of your dreams. I am the angel of your soul and the compass for your destiny. I will give your heart wings."*

"Hello, my soul," the princess replied. "Every night I seek your appearance. Every day

I honor my destiny." Princess Angilika was elated to receive a rare glimpse into her soul, and her heart was filled with gladness. She finally discovered that the Angel of the Eastern Star was the heavenly being that lived within her soul and was the voice of her dreams.

The Divine Prophecy from the Art Gods

Struggling to keep the spell upon her, the Phantom Prophet hastened the magic mirror to prophesy her destiny. *"The art gods have chosen you, Princess Angilika. You have been favored to spread artistic inspiration and goodwill to all peoples of the third millennium. You shall possess supernatural powers to accomplish this incredible mission. Graces shall be bestowed upon you, for your soul shall then be born immortal and will live on beyond the horizons of all time."* Upon hearing the words of her divine prophecy, the princess became overwhelmed with excitement …then, her heart skipped a beat.

Suddenly!! Poof!! The trance was broken and the princess was elevated back to her feet. Distressed that the trance had ended so quickly, she became instantly disturbed. She then realized that even her supreme happiness stood in the way of her quest to learn the truth. How confused she was!

"Dear Father! This can't be all there is! I demand to know more!" Princess Angilika cried out to the king.

"SORCERER! REVEAL WHAT YOU KNOW!" demanded the king in a furious voice.

Fearing the king's wrath, the Phantom Prophet replied with a powerful prophecy that raised the king's concern. The king listened intently and shifted uneasily in his throne. The princess had tears in her eyes and the queen trembled with anticipation.

The Almighty Centurion Genie Revealed

Continuing in a trembling voice, the Phantom Prophet revealed a spiritual secret. "Your princess must release the angel of her soul, and this will not be an easy task. For this to happen, she must be granted supernatural powers from the art gods. Hence, you must seek the Almighty Centurion Genie that dwells inside a magical lantern made of gold, laden with jewels and precious stones. He is the only one in all the kingdoms who possesses the superpowers to fulfill the prophecy the art gods have set forth this dark evening. Indeed, My Lord, this genie is not easily available to just anyone, for many thieves desire the Almighty Centurion Genie's powers to curse the lands with evil. But for you, My Lord, I will reveal where to find him."

An Impossible Journey

The prophet continued his spiritual instructions. "Your messengers must search the ends of every rainbow in all kingdoms far and wide. At the end of one special rainbow there are five dancing leprechauns destined to protect a large pot of gold. Inside this golden pot dwells a powerful genie and his magnificent golden lantern. This powerful genie has been destined to obey Princess Angilika. Until you discover the treasure of this rainbow and crown Princess Angilika as the Mistress of the Almighty Centurion Genie, the angel of her soul shall never be released."

The princess looked at the prophet with tears streaming down her cheeks. She felt the mixed emotions of grave disappointment and heightened gladness, all at the same time. With courage, she said to him, "You have given me hope within a brief moment of divine revelation. You have strengthened my faith in the beliefs I hold deeply. I shall cherish this divine prophecy deep within my heart forever. I shall never forget you."

Knowing that he could say no more, and fearing the king's repeated commands, the Phantom Prophet quickly rushed away to his home back in the desert.

CHAPTER FOUR

Marko, the Marvelous Magician

Disappointed that it may take years to find this lantern, or worse yet, that it would never be found, Princess Angilika threw herself down at her father's feet and began to weep. Her heart was heavy with disappointment. But she also knew that she had to cheer up and keep striving for truth and purpose, even through the difficult test of time she was about to confront.

Filled with compassion at the sight of his daughter's distress, he knew he had to do something. Immediately, the king summoned the kingdom's magician named Marko. He was the fastest messenger of all the palace servants and was widely known for his clever disappearing acts and wild storytelling. But he was also notorious for his occasional irresponsible and careless deeds.

Hearing that he was summoned by King Melchior, Marko the Marvelous quickly arrived at the castle, hastily ushered in by the castle servants. He knelt before the royal family and said, "I am here, My Lord. What wild stories of legends or clever magic tricks shall I entertain you with this day?"

The king smiled back, but immediately became very stoic. The magician sensed that the king was not happy. He glanced over at the princess and saw her sadness. Filled with compassion Marko said, "I can make you smile today, my pretty one. Please don't cry. I don't like to see you cry."

The king wasted no time on small talk and began the instructions for his rule. King Melchior relayed the prophecy of the art gods for his daughter's destiny and the Phantom's spiritual instructions for an impossible journey. The king gave Marko the royal command to search

the ends of every rainbow in all the kingdoms near and far to find the five dancing leprechauns.

"Marko, you shall seek and find the Almighty Centurion Genie that lives inside this magic lantern! Hurry! Make haste now! Bring it back to me, and I will richly reward you with a house of gold to perform your tricks."

"This is a great mission for you, Marko, but you must return as quickly as the days go by. Our precious princess struggles every day and every night with her quest for truth and purpose. Perhaps you can be the one to help find the answers to her destiny."

As Marko turned to leave, the king gave him a stern warning. "I am entrusting you with a mission that will demand great sacrifice and sincere devotion to its cause. Marko! Cast off all your human imperfections! The princess shall be awaiting your return every single day from this moment forward."

Receiving the royal command, Marko hurried off, hoping that he would gain favor from the king and be the victorious one to retrieve the magic lantern with the Centurion Genie inside. Marko really wanted to help the beautiful princess discover the answers to her destiny. So, before he rushed off into the kingdom, Marko told Angilika another wild story about flying carpets and shooting stars. The princess smiled and imagined herself and Queenie traveling the kingdoms on a flying carpet.

As Marko left the castle gates, he turned around to see the princess waving back at him. This time she had a hopeful smile on her face. But still, she doubted Marko and questioned herself. *"Does he really have what it takes to challenge the hardships of this mission? How long is this going to take?"* She thought with resolve. *"Can I now remain steadfast throughout the test of time and never grow weary of dreaming?"*

Princess Angilika continued to live her playful daydreams and to sleep her happy night dreams for many years after that last goodbye to Marko. However, little did she know that these countless dreams were forecasting her destiny to the immortal missions that the art gods had in store for her in the Third Millennium.

CHAPTER FIVE

The Magic Golden Lantern Discovered

Now it came to pass that almost thirty years had come and gone, and still Marko had not returned. But every day and every night were filled with happy dreams for the princess. However, Princess Angilika was saddened to believe he may have gotten lost, and remained hopeful every day that her destiny would someday appear in the stars. She had never forgotten the divine prophecy delivered by the Phantom Prophet from the art gods, nor the inspiring eyes of the most beautiful angel-being within her soul.

Then, one ordinary day while feeding the swans, Princess Angilika caught a glimpse of a very colorful figure hastily running toward the palace gardens. *"Was that Marko?"* she thought. *"And what does he have in his arms?"* As the figure drew nearer, she recognized him immediately! "OPEN THE GATES AT ONCE!" she screamed. "Let this man come to the throne of King Melchior," commanded Princess Angilika to the gate servants.

Rushing as fast as he could, Marko was quickly ushered to the throne of King Melchior. His pace had quickened, for he couldn't wait another day to make the princess happy. The princess followed with great anticipation. Queen Helena also hurried to the throne as soon as she found out that Marko had finally returned.

After all had gathered around the throne, the king sarcastically inquired, "What took you so long, Marko? My daughter had dreams every night and every day that you would return with the revelation of her destiny. Your delay has caused our princess much grief. I hope that on this day you shall reward the princess's patience."

"I beg your forgiveness, My Lord, that it took so many years for me to return. Indeed, not only do I have a wild story to tell," remarked Marko, "but I have a magical surprise for our princess!"

Proudly, Marko reached inside his traveling bag and presented a magnificent lantern made of solid gold, sparkling with jewels and precious stones, and placed it at the king's feet. Its radiance glistened, just like the glorious rays of its rainbow home. It immediately captivated everyone's attention and no one could take their eyes off its glimmering beauty.

All at once, Marko aroused his storytelling charms! He could not wait to begin telling the long wild story about the many distressing adventures of his travels, which took him to every kingdom in the Orient. He told stories of how he impatiently waited for any rainbow to appear, and even made up new magic tricks to make rain so that a rainbow would form. Then when one finally appeared, he would set out to search for its end, but never found anything!

Then came the good news…"One day, My Lord, I approached from afar and saw a very odd-looking rainbow with shooting sparkles of gold, silver, and copper glistening between its colorful rays. I knew for sure that this was something I had never seen before. I searched days for the end of this rainbow, putting my life in grave danger. I even had to travel through a dark and deserted forest filled with witches and trolls. But suddenly, I was taken captive by the Lonely Witch of Darkness. I was forced to entertain her with magic tricks and wild stories. In fact, I was detained there for years in a giant tree fort guarded below by hungry wolves. Indeed, My Lord, I tried to escape every day, but the witch's brew intoxicated me into a story frenzy."

Slightly amused by his exaggerated story, the king glanced at his princess daughter and Queen Helena, giving them a broad smile.

Marko continued in an excited voice that made him talk very fast. "Finally, by the luck of one of those little green leprechauns, I got the chance to perform a classic disappearing act that led to my escape! In no time at all, I spotted the end! As fast as I could, I ran to the end of this magnificent rainbow, and to my surprise, discovered the five green leprechauns dancing around a giant pot of gold. The leprechauns were singing and dancing in a circle, holding hands and jumping for joy. Three of them were tall and the other two were much smaller. I then commanded the five, 'The lantern that lies within this pot of gold must be turned over to King Melchior immediately!'"

Knowing King Melchior's reputation over all the lands for being highly respected and honorable, the leprechauns happily surrendered the lantern to Marko, entrusting its powers to be used for the good of mankind. They immediately ran off to play their games, jubilant that they had fulfilled their destiny and no longer had to guard the Almighty Centurion Genie and his luxurious magic lantern.

"I wasted no time, My Lord, but it took me ten more years to get back to your kingdom. The lonely witch tried to follow me so that she could rub the lantern and use it for her evil deeds. So I had to travel in circles and cover up my tracks to get rid of her," finished the magician as he took a deep breath.

Once his wild storytelling had ended, Marko sighed with relief and beamed with pride as he presented the golden magic lantern to Princess Angilika. Honoring his promise to reward the magician, the king commanded his bricklayers to build a house of gold in the center of the kingdom's courtyard for Marko the Marvelous Magician.

CHAPTER SIX

The Almighty Centurion Genie

While all marveled at the beauty of this golden lantern, Princess Angilika moved closer to the steps of her father's throne, anticipating what was going to come next. Feeling the excitement and sudden rush of her destiny upon her, she thought, *"This must be what destiny feels like when it draws near, for I have waited so long and have never felt like this before!"* At the same time, she sensed relief that her battles and struggles might finally be over. She glorified the moment, because she knew that in the very next moment, she would receive the ultimate reward for her courage and fortitude. And all the answers she sought to the mysteries of her destiny would now be revealed.

Just then, a fast wind blew in and swirled around the lantern and disappeared inside. Its momentary fury announced the arrival of powerful heavenly forces from the art gods. All present honored this divine sign from the heavens and bowed their heads with respect. The crowd pressed forward. Small children squeezed their way to the front to get a better view. The Phantom Prophet heard the news, too, but stayed hidden in the crowd. Even Marko couldn't believe his own eyes, for surely he knew this wasn't one of his magic tricks. Queenie, imitating Angilika with outstretched wings, welcomed with respect the divine truth sent down from the art gods.

Capturing the moment of his daughter's destiny and fulfilling the Phantom Prophet's spiritual instructions, the king knew what he had to do. King Melchior stood in their midst and raised the golden lantern with outstretched arms over his loving daughter. Wielding his royal powers, the king proclaimed in a loud voice that was heard by all. "I CROWN YOU, PRINCESS ANGILIKA, AS MISTRESS OF THE ALMIGHTY

CENTURION GENIE THAT DWELLS WITHIN THIS GOLDEN LANTERN. THE ART GODS HAVE SPOKEN!"

Slowly, King Melchoir descended the steps and set the golden lantern down in front of Angilika. With a tear in his eye, he knew his precious daughter was now betrothed. Queen Helena was moved with joy. It was a glorious moment to behold!

The princess sensed what was going to come next. She had dreams of this moment since hearing her divine prophecy from the magic mirror. It was one of her most frequent dreams that always seemed to keep her in a deep, happy sleep. She already knew what to do. Instinctively, she removed its seal and rubbed the lantern three times. Then she said in a forceful voice, "OH, ALMIGHTY CENTURION GENIE, I COMMAND YOU TO APPEAR AT ONCE! MANIFEST YOUR POWERS BEFORE ME! YOU HAVE BEEN DESTINED TO OBEY ONLY ME."

Suddenly, the lantern began to rumble and small puffs of white mist started to spiral outward. Large billows of incense followed, gushing forth with great force. Sweet fragrances of precious oils filled the air. Its magical mist, raining down upon the entire rotunda and sparkling with flakes of gold and silver, settled upon the golden hair of Princess Angilika. The mighty rush of royal air continued to swirl around and around like a giant whirlwind, lastly forming itself into the shape of a monstrous genie. Suddenly, before her eyes appeared the Almighty Centurion Genie in all his glory. King Melchior and Queen Helena were spellbound by the awesome sight before them!

Enchanted with delight, Princess Angilika gazed upon him with reverence. Her powerful genie was ten feet tall, dark-skinned, with bushy eyebrows and black hair. He had gentle brown eyes, and his robes of white silk were tied with ropes made of gold and silver threads. Tassels of jewels dangled with elegance, proclaiming his Oriental glory. He held a dazzling silver sword in one hand and an embossed copper shield in the other.

"Oh, my beautiful Mistress Angilika," the genie responded with servitude. "I have been sent to you by powerful art gods. I have waited millennia for your commands, and my powers have been magnified by the passage of time. The angel of your soul shall be released, and your soul shall become an immortal spirit for the good of all mankind. The art gods have instructed me to bestow upon you the superpowers which only I possess. You have much to accomplish, but with my powers, you shall instill artistic inspiration, joy, and goodwill over all the lands…and to all its peoples…anywhere you go." "COMMAND ME, MY MISTRESS."

"Oh, my Almighty Centurion Genie…" her fluttering voice started to speak. Feeling breathless, she recalled divine messages that the Phantom Prophet revealed almost thirty years ago. So, with a loud, commanding voice, she announced, "TRANSPORT MY IMMORTAL SOUL…TO THE DAYS OF THE THIRD MILLENNIUM…BESTOW UPON ME YOUR SUPER POWERS…THAT I MAY FULFILL MY DESTINY AND LIVE MY TRUE IDENTITY."

"My lovely mistress," the genie responded. "You did not realize that from the beginning of your soul's existence, you were already living your true identity. You have handcrafted royal garments since you were gifted from birth. You have brought joy to your royal parents and to all those who have encountered your beautiful countenance. And your compassionate and generous spirit has lifted even the lowliest of handmaidens." The princess stood spellbound at the commanding sound of her genie's voice. She was touched by his loving embrace.

"You shall now be rewarded for the honest life you live," the wise genie continued. "In your quest for truth and purpose, you have endured the hauntings of your dreams that only brought you frustration and sadness. You have overcome fear and disappointment in the grave face of danger. You remained steadfast amid the endless tests of time, even though you grew weary awaiting the answers to your destiny. You have sustained many hardships. You have maintained courage and hope throughout the many battles between good and evil that constantly prevailed during your life. Princess Angilika, the art gods have chosen you."

The genie took a deep breath and paused for a moment. He leaned downward, smiled gently, and crossed his heart with his giant strong arms. The Almighty Centurion Genie looked deeply into the beautiful eyes of his mistress and spoke slowly and reverently, breathing upon her with every word. "WITH ME…YOU SHALL NOW FIND…TRUTH AND PURPOSE…FOR WHICH YOU HAVE DILIGENTLY SOUGHT… ALL YOUR LIFE."

The Rapture Exchange

Suddenly, Princess Angilika fell forward, limp, and right into the protective arms of her Centurion Genie. Beads of sweat formed on her forehead. She felt breathless and faint again. The magnetic forces of his superpowers upon transferring into her body were mighty, warm, and embracing. He was truly the most powerful man she had ever met in her entire life.

There was not a sound that could be heard in the room. The people were silent. No one stirred. Dare they move? They had just witnessed the powerful transfer of rapture from the Almighty Centurion Genie to Princess Angilika. Rays of sunshine fell upon the princess's golden hair and beamed across the rotunda from the castle windows above. Garden butterflies, attracted to the flowery incense, danced in the sunlit beams. Songbirds flew in from the sculpture gardens and filled the air with music. Everyone there was paralyzed with awe, and all eyes were fixed upon the monstrous genie and the little princess.

The Centurion Genie gently lifted Princess Angilika to the level of his eyes once again and steadied her position. She returned his glance and fixed her eyes upon his for the second time. This time, she peered deeply into his soul, and he peered back into hers. Princess Angilika remained spellbound and motionless in the giant genie's arms as his rapture claimed her heart. Their bond was instantly magnetic and alluring!

Suddenly and very quickly, he rose high above her. Magnifying his powers inside the magical trance he placed upon Angilika, his deep, masculine voice broke the silence. "YOUR DESTINY IS MY ROAD MAP, MY BEAUTIFUL MISTRESS. But first, I must bestow upon you my genie super tools to ensure that the missions of your destiny will perpetuate your soul for eternity. Receive now these instruments of power."

He raised his silver sword and waved it over the lantern as he beckoned the release of a golden needle. "This magic sewing needle possesses great powers. With this golden needle, you shall create the most beautiful garments in the world. Your garments will be desired by many." Princess Angilika smiled as she received the golden needle from the genie, anticipating its magical possibilities. She envisioned all the beautiful garments that she would forever make.

Then again with the same wave of motions over the lantern, he beckoned the release of a heart-shaped locket made of solid gold. The genie said, "The days of the third millennium will not be a happy time, but your generosity shall always prevail. Within this golden heart locket, joy and goodwill shall be plentiful for you to bestow upon everyone you meet." She took the locket and safeguarded it gently around her neck.

The genie continued, "Your missions in the third millennium will encounter many hardships, but you shall endure all adversity. However, your own precious heart must also flourish in happiness. To this end, I will transport your magic pet swan, Queenie, to be your secret confidant all the days of your eternity. She will provide endless joy and gladness to carry you through your days of trial."

The genie raised his sword above his head again, then flashed it back and forth erratically over the princess with large circular motions. With a sudden burst of magical energy, her beautiful black-necked swan was magically transformed into a swan vesture of armor to keep the princess

safe throughout her long journey through time. Everyone watching was captivated by the fascination of this magic genie. In the next moment he pronounced a legend for all to bear witness.

The Prophecy of the Almighty Centurion Genie

"You will enter the third millennium and land upon a tranquil crystal pond. There, this beautiful creature shall reign with elegance and grace as the Fantasy Swan to ensure your unending happiness. None can be more wondrous than your Queenie."

"On this landing spot, my magic spell upon Queenie will end and the swan vesture you are wearing will transform back into your magical pet swan. In this defining moment, the angel of your soul shall be released, and you will finally discover your soul's identity and your purpose for birth. All peoples of the third millennium who gaze upon the fantastic aura of this magic swan shall ponder their own soulful revelation that will move their hearts to joy."

Bewildered, but enchanted, the princess looked down on her body and saw that she was no longer wearing the princess dress she had made. It was gone. In its place, she was wearing a magical swan vesture of armor. *"It's beautiful!"* she thought. *"I'm really wearing Queenie!"* Again, the princess was amazed at the powerful strength of the genie's powers and the gentleness of his loving nature.

CHAPTER SEVEN

The Magic Umbrella and the Flying Magic Carpet

By now, an even larger crowd had gathered quietly in the rotunda. Even with this many people, not a sound or stirring could be heard. The awesome sight of this magnificent giant standing before the kingdom's only princess had captured everyone into a motionless spell of magical energy. The enchanting mystery that prevailed in the air was more than they had anticipated. They couldn't wait for more!

The genie continued his bestowals, but reached down for Queen Helena's umbrella. "At last, my beautiful Mistress, to protect you from all danger, I present to you this magic umbrella armor. Under it, no harm shall ever befall you. You must carry it on your journey and everywhere you go."

Princess Angilika was glad that the genie gave her a magic umbrella. Of all her childhood memories, this was one of her favorite pastimes…she had always pretended to play whispering games with the angels under the sheltering shield of her mother's umbrella.

Now, the princess was so excited that she could hardly wait to leave. However, she paused abruptly with a hesitation that disturbed her. The princess questioned the genie with great concern. "But Almighty Centurion Genie, how will I get to the third millennium? How far is it? The Phantom Prophet prophesied that I must possess your superpowers to instill artistic inspiration and goodwill inside the souls…of all peoples… of all lands. How will I accomplish this incredible feat?"

Immediately, the Centurion Genie laughed with a very mischievous and crooked smile. Raising his dark, bushy eyebrows at the thought of how he was going to get his Mistress to the third millennium, he snickered. "Hmmm, I think we could have a little fun here!"

"The days of the third millennium are very far away. But your soul is now immortal, and with my powers, you shall arrive swiftly and safely. You will travel through several time warps and galaxies, and you shall arrive with elegance and beauty." Princess Angilika's interest perked up as she anxiously waited for the Almighty Centurion Genie to finish speaking.

Suddenly, the princess felt an odd sensation creep upon her. The hair on her head tingled. The hair on her arms raised, and she could feel her heart beating faster. Her toes felt warm and tingling, too. In fact, her whole body felt like it was submerged under a giant wave of magnetic energy. *"What was that?"* she thought. *"He is so strong!"*

Sensing that his powers were finally taking over the princess, and knowing he had much more to accomplish, the Almighty Centurion Genie repositioned himself for more supernatural deeds. He continued, "Your father's throne is adorned with the most magnificent carpets at his feet because you made them. Now, one of them will take you on a wild ride to the 3rd millennium. Your travels shall always be swift and smooth."

Princess Angilika looked down and remembered this beautiful velvet carpet trimmed with gold tassels. It was one of many she had made especially for her father. But, before the princess could look back up at her father, the genie's superpowers took over! He briskly waved his silver sword again in a circular motion over the carpet. Suddenly, the same magical mist sparkling with silver and gold flakes appeared like a thick valley fog. But this time, the scents of incense were overpowering. The carpet began to shudder and flutter lightly, coming to life on its own! Its sudden movement captured the princess off guard. She almost fell off. Gently, the velvet carpet slowly lifted upward with a soft puff and poof. Waiting for the genie's command, it hovered high above the rotunda floor.

The Coronation of "AngiArts"

With a commanding voice, the Almighty Centurion Genie announced her coronation. *"Your flying magic carpet will transport you anywhere your missions take you. It is woven with the supernatural powers of the art gods. It shall never fail you. You will float and glide with beauty and elegance over all the lands. Your destiny has been determined since your soul has been in existence. With my superpowers, you are destined to instill artistic inspiration into all cultures of the third millennium and beyond. **AND YOU SHALL BE KNOWN AS "ANGIARTS."***"

CHAPTER EIGHT

The Journey to the Third Millennium

In all its magical glory, the magic carpet began to slowly rise higher and higher until it almost touched the dome ceiling. Stunned by its magnificent aura, everyone below gazed upward to witness the fantastic phenomenon. King Melchior had a proud tear in his eye. Queen Helena smiled and waved goodbye. She had waited so long to finally see that her beautiful daughter was on her way to fulfill her true destiny. "I love you, my precious daughter!" the queen blurted out. "GODSPEED!"

As quick as a flash…with a hissing swish and a loud, mighty swoosh… the Almighty Centurion Genie disintegrated and disappeared back into his magic lantern, preparing himself for the long journey ahead and to wait for commands from his beautiful Mistress. "*I can't wait to see her again,*" he thought as he settled within his small lantern home. "*She is the most beautiful woman to whom I could ever want to bestow my magical powers.*"

Meanwhile, as the red royal carpet hovered above, vibrating with magical energy, Princess Angilika recalled Marko's wild legend of flying carpets and shooting stars. This was another moment she dreamed about, and even this one was now about to come true!

Just then, she heard a familiar voice from within her soul whispering, "Get ready! Your time has come." She recognized it to be the sweet voice of the Angel of the Eastern Star and a compass for the journeys to her destiny. "*I will need my angel's wings,*" she thought.

The magic carpet abruptly accelerated forward, maneuvering toward a very large window in the Great Clay Castle's walls. With another loud swoosh, the carpet took off, leaving a sparkling trail of silver and

gold flakes streaming back onto Queen Helena's hair. Princess Angilika looked at the bright shining sky ahead of her and noticed that her journey had started with a wild flight back over the rainbow where Marko had discovered her genie's lantern. "How radiant and colorful it is!" she thought. She quickly glanced below to the fast-moving landscape and noticed the five leprechauns dancing around and waving back. "Thank you for guarding my genie and his golden lantern home," she called out to them.

As Mistress "AngiArts" was swiftly whisked away on her journey to the third millennium, the whole kingdom of King Melchior celebrated with the royal family. Sublimely, the Angel of the Eastern Star pronounced in a heavenly voice that resonated throughout the kingdom:

"You can claim your true identity!
Like an angel upon the wings of God,
flying headlong into the divine nature
of your innermost being.
Where you are free to believe in your dreams
and trust your imaginings.
Free to grasp hold of that which you can only be.
Free, at last, to live your destiny!"

THE END

CHAPTER NINE
Follow the Monument Map

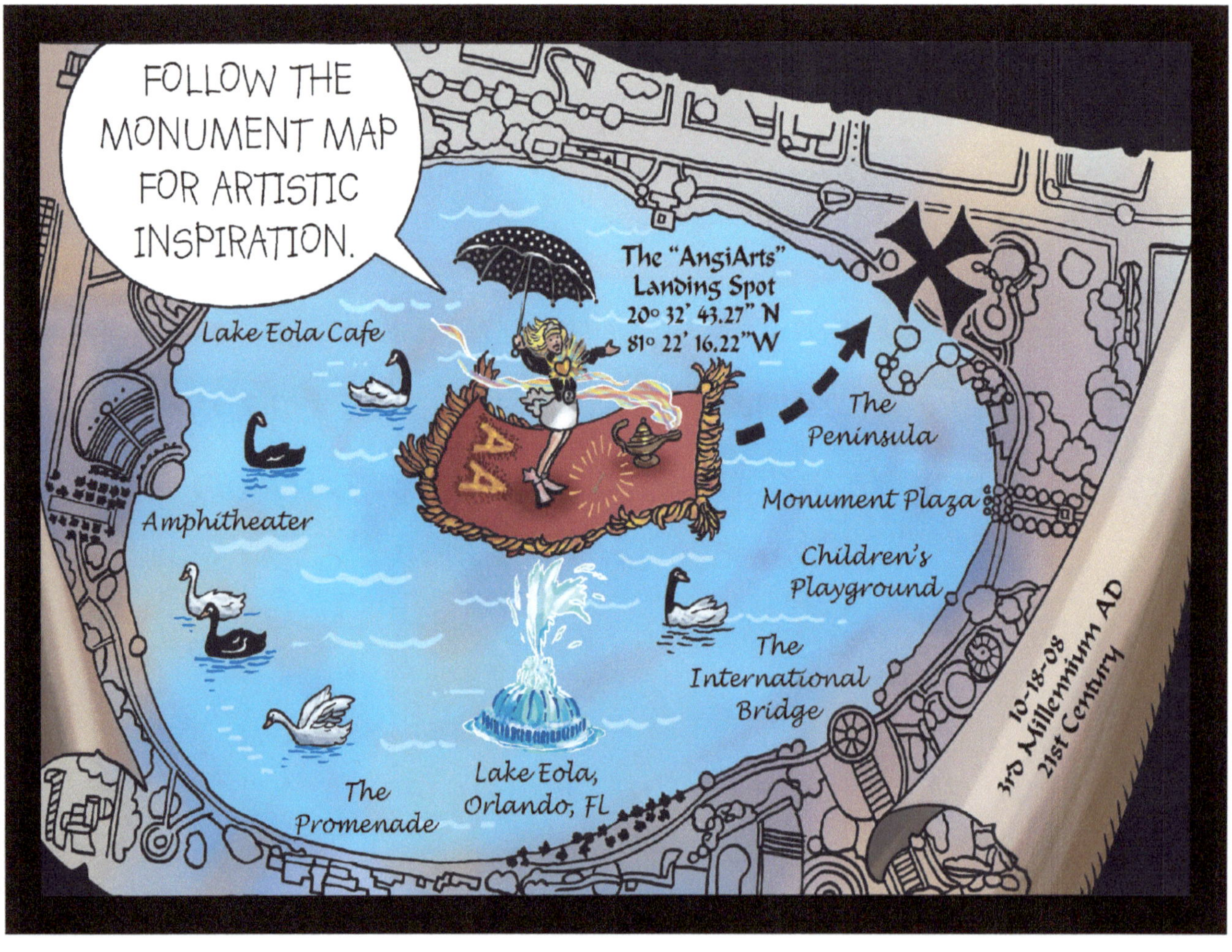

A MONUMENT FOR ARTISTIC INSPIRATION

"AngiArts" invites all Peoples of the Third Millennium to behold the superpowers of the Almighty Centurion Genie. Your mission is to delve into an individual quest for soulful self-prophecy, and to *"hold the trance"* for an interactive literary theatre experience as you follow the Monument Map to the "AngiArts" legendary landing spot at Lake Eola.

Believe in magic for just a moment and challenge your senses to *watch* fantasy unfold to reality right before your very eyes. As per the preceding story---the landing spot portrays the magical moment that the swan vesture is transformed back into a black-necked swan as the angel of the princess' soul is released.

As you gaze upon The Fantasy Swan and the magical moment it evokes, may the superpowers of the Almighty Centurion Genie lead you to an unimaginable revelation in your life.

LETTERBOOK NOTES

What is your soulful revelation that moves your heart to joy?

_____
_____
_____
_____
_____
_____
_____
_____
_____
_____

LETTERBOOK NOTES

Who is your true identity?

_____

_____

_____

_____

_____

_____

_____

_____

_____

CONCLUSION

Introducing a perpetually adventurous muse, this creative tale fabricates the fantastic reality of Orlando's *first-ever* cartoon character for the Arts, on a mission to inspire the cultural history of the City Beautiful. Charming onlookers and patrons to enrich their theatre experiences, "AngiArts" is an impassioned art zealot with superpowers, who may unexpectedly "appear" atop downtown Orlando's skyscrapers or rove about its cultural landscape from time to time as she continues the missions of her destiny. She infuses artistic adventure and comical fantasy in her own way.

The missions of her destiny in the third millennium begin in downtown Orlando and cannot be accomplished without the artistic involvement and collaboration of its community.

With her Golden Needle, "AngiArts" will handcraft the costumes for the premiere performance of <u>The Identity of "AngiArts"</u>—rewritten for a live theatre production. With lots of "genie-magic," it would be produced locally and presented at the future venue of the magnificent Dr. Phillips Performing Arts Center 2012, currently under construction. Certainly, this creative endeavor would involve the expert knowledge and services of many theatre professionals.

Joy and goodwill are plentiful inside her Golden Locket. "AngiArts" spreads friendship and smiles to the less fortunate with "Socks of Happiness"™ from her sister identity, "Bluebird Cinderella."™ Transporting goodwill wherever it needs to flourish, the generosity of a community always prevails.

"AngiArts" carries her Magic Umbrella everywhere she goes, unifying all facets of our arts community under an umbrella of artistic inspiration. Collaborating with highly creative, ambitious cartoon artists, "AA" is on

a mission to create animated pep rallies and townspeople comic strips. This dynamic effort may present the arts community with a humorous and informative platform to communicate with Central Florida patrons.

The flying Magic Carpet transports "AngiArts" to anywhere her missions take her. In addition to the other identities of the "*Walking~Works~of~Art*" collection, "AngiArts" beckons viewers to embrace the magical value of imagination for visual arts that *"walk around,"* spontaneously appearing at cultural venues around town. Any patron could be a *walking work of art* if one creates it so. You might be hand-picked by the art gods.

The incredible mission of "AngiArts" is to rally a momentous and interactive Arts—Culture—Literature Movement across our City Beautiful, while commanding the Almighty Centurion Genie to unleash his superpowers to all facets of our arts and culture community. To boldly forecast the future of Orlando's cultural climate is to predict a dynamic flurry of artistic inspiration—not only as we Orlandoans await the grand openings of three major art venues, but as residents and visitors alike make downtown's sidewalks resonate with the energetic rhythm of their entertainment adventures.

Today, "AngiArts" celebrates and joins the collective efforts of our vibrant arts community, which includes all leaders of the City Beautiful and the numerous arts and cultural resources, organizations, and patrons who continuously cultivate Orlando's cultural ambience. Together, we are presenting a world-class *City for the Arts* to central Floridians and to all honored visitors from around the world.

Tomorrow, "I claim to say: Our cultures evolve by the stories we tell. If you don't write them down, then what will you leave behind?"—**A.P.**

CHARACTER EVOLUTION OF "AngiArts"

Press Release Info Dated September 29, 2008
Lake Eola Orlando Florida

Initially conceived as a caricature of herself, Angi Perretti contrived the character of "AngiArts"© in 2006 to rally and promote the arts and culture movement in downtown Orlando. The caricature is a combination of fantasy genre and a mixture of cartoon elements. She flies around on her magic red-theatre carpet and delivers "genie magic" wherever it is needed.

This identity personality came into my thoughts as I was thinking about how I would fabricate a humorous caricature of myself. This endeavor eventually evolved to become a very rewarding, yet, a most daring project for me. The character that surfaced from my imagination was one that may be considered a cross-mix between the 20th century comic book characters--Superman, Batman, Betty Boop, Wonder Woman, and Dick Tracy.

Enthralled with cartoons that made me laugh when I was a child, I decided that my character could be like one of those, but at the same time, portray virtuous ideals to her existence--The Ideals which include the goodness of heart that artistic creativity and imagination bring to the souls of our youth; The ideals that promote the expansion of literature, alongside humor, fun, and wit to our daily lives. And, lastly, the ideals of fantasy and charm that entice us to a reality escape into our own *"classroom of self-discovery."*

Soon after, I designed a zany *Betty-Boop-like*, hot pink dress with black polka dots for the photo shoot. "AA" made her Premier Appearance at a charity event, "Oscar Night America," on March 5, 2006 at the Rosen Centre Hotel. Two months later, I published the "AngiArts"© trademark identity in May, 2006 issue, Page 3, in the Orlando Arts Magazine.

It wasn't until two years later that I resurrected a literary project to "breathe" life into this identity. I wanted to fabricate a story about her and to give her an origin background to which readers and fans could relate. The story incorporates universal themes about our human struggles; the regrets and disappointments we so often face; and our unanimous desires for hopes and dreams we cherish so deeply. OH…and, let's not forget to mention the superhuman missions we all might imagine ourselves doing at one time or another. Right? **A.P.**

"CARICATURE OF THE AUTHOR"

"AngiArts" Comic Strip 2008

A Future Art Project for Talented and Ambitious Illustrators

AUTHOR PROFILE

Angi Perretti was born on December 23, 1951, and lived an idyllic childhood on a remote ten-acre farm in rural Miami, Florida, with two nurturing parents. Joe and Helen Muscare named the farm, "Happy Acres." Angi spent many playful outdoor hours confiding in her pet horses, cows and rabbits and building tree forts with her older brother, Mark. It was here at the age of thirteen that she was first inspired to become a costume designer. By then, it was the mid '60s and a constant fantasy of hers was to create costumes for Elvis and Cher. One day, Angi's mother showed her how to sew a pair of shorts. From that day forward, her natural talent flourished.

In her twenties, she designed and created fancy shirts and stage outfits for country-western bands. She also custom made band uniforms for an entire high school majorette team in Immokalee, Florida. In 1978, she founded Bikini Creations in Deerfield Beach, Florida—a custom-made swimwear boutique for models and beauty pageants. Just after they were married on November 18, 1978, she and her BIG Italian husband, Nick Perretti, founded Mr. Deli Restaurant in Florida City, Florida, on July 4, 1981.

The Perretti's moved to Orlando and founded the PerriHouse Bed & Breakfast Inn at Lake Buena Vista on May 1, 1989. There, they enjoyed thirteen years of entertaining people from all over the world right at their breakfast table. On January 20, 2006, Angi realized a childhood dream of a lifetime and founded her costume design studio at Cottage Way in the Lake Eola Heights Historic District of downtown Orlando. A family flag pole monument stands at the corner of Summerlin Avenue and Amelia Street. On October 18, 2008, Angi founded the "Fantasy Swan Monument" at Lake Eola—Orlando's Monument for Artistic Inspiration.

As a costume designer and master seamstress, Angi defines her artistic inspirations with a human identity, portraying each unique character and personality within the silhouettes and fabrics of her designs. The *"Walking-Works-of-Art"*™ collection of trademark designs represents her elegant perspectives and tasteful expressions of the visual arts—

The Chronicles of Angi Perretti ©

ARTIST STATEMENT

"WALKING~WORKS~OF~ART"

Angi Perretti—Costume Designer and Artist, displays her "Walking~Works~of~Art" upon the human figure by a signature portrait of fabrics and colors via haute couture. Available for viewing only a short time—as an eclipse of art—the viewers of Angi's artwork should consider themselves hand-picked by the art gods with a divine invitation to ponder an artistic moment of wonder and diversion. Incidentally, if you didn't get to see her, you'll never know what you missed.

But if you do---like it or not—it's art!

www.ingramcontent.com/pod-product-compliance
Lightning Source LLC
Chambersburg PA
CBHW042139290426
44110CB00002B/60